An A&C Bla

CU00409684

GREAT
Space Songs

TOPICAL SONGS FOR SCHOOLS

CD/CD-ROM
NO MUSIC READING REQUIRED
WHITEBOARD POPUPS
AND FULL AUDIO SUPPORT

Selected and arranged
by Stephen Chadwick

Performed by
Kim Chandler, Cleveland Watkiss,
Anthony Strong and Kaz Simmons

A & C Black • London

SUN BLAST

SING
It's a spinning ball of gas,
Want to know more, then just ask,
Twinkle, twinkle shining star,
I'm wondering what you are.

How you dazzle with your light,
You're the Sun that's burning bright,
Twinkle, twinkle shining star,
I'm wondering what you are.

RAP
The Sun is huge, as you can see,
With many times earth's gravity.
Its solar wind and magnetism
Extend across the solar system.

What makes up our shining Sun?
Seems it's mostly hydrogen
(Some helium and little more)
With nuclear fusion at its core.

SING
Ninety-three million miles away,
Just one star in the Milky Way ~
Hello Mister Sun:

It's a spinning ball of gas…

RAP
The surface of the Sun is hot:
Six thousand degrees, I kid you not!
The light shines from this photosphere
And takes eight minutes to reach us here.

Its atmosphere is even hotter,
Extending into space it's got a
Chromosphere, a corona and that's
Millions of degrees so you all wear your sun hats.

SING
Ninety-three million miles away…

It's a spinning ball of gas…

RAP
So hydrogen's the nuclear fuel
That keeps the Sun from going cool.
With all that fusion going on,
One day this fuel will all be gone.

So stick around five billion years,
The Sun will start to disappear.
I know what you're thinking, for what it's worth,
That would be the end of planet Earth!

SING
It's a spinning ball of gas…

▶ **CD** track 1 (performance) track 2 (backing) track 3 (teaching)
▶ **CD-ROM**: audio-embedded lyrics/melody; slide show; lesson plan; piano accompaniment

FOOTPRINTS ON THE MOON

INTRODUCTION ~ astronauts talking on the moon

CHORUS

I'm stepping on the Moon,
I'm walking on the Moon,
I'm leaving footprints on the Moon.

VERSE

Craters large and small betray a violent history,
Ancient lava flows that spread to form
   the rocky seas,
And on the near side, tranquillity,
Around the far side is mystery
As I leave my footprints on the Moon.

LUNAR DANCE ~ astronauts talking

Footprints
Footprints in the lunar dust,
Footprints
Footprints on the Moon,
Footprints
Footprints in the lunar dust,
Footprints
Footprints on the Moon.

CHORUS

I'm stepping on the Moon,
I'm walking on the Moon,
I'm leaving footprints on the Moon.

VERSE

Up above the Moon's horizon, coming into view,
Earth is floating in a starless sky – green and blue,
So many miles to journey here,
I stand so lonely upon this sphere
As I leave my footprints on the Moon.

LUNAR DANCE ~ astronauts talking

Footprints
Footprints in the lunar dust,
Footprints
Footprints on the Moon,
Footprints
Footprints in the lunar dust,
Footprints
Footprints on the Moon.

CHORUS

I'm stepping on the Moon…

VERSE

Lunar gravity is pulling Earth from side to side,
Lifting up the oceans, dragging them to make the tides,
The Moon in orbit, a satellite,
Waxing and waning, throughout the nights
As I leave my footprints on the Moon.

WHISPERED

Footprints on the Moon.

▶ CD track 4
(performance)
track 5 (backing)
track 6 (teaching: verse)
track 7 (teaching:
lunar dance counting)

▶ CD-ROM: audio-
embedded lyrics
and melody; slide
show; movie;
lesson plan; piano
accompaniment

5

THE GALAXY SONG

Just remember that you're standing on a planet that's evolving,
Revolving at nine hundred miles an hour,
It's orbiting at nineteen miles a second, so it's reckoned,
A sun that is the source of all our power.
The Sun and you and me and all the stars that we can see
Are moving at a million miles a day,
In an outer spiral arm, at forty thousand miles an hour,
Of the galaxy we call the 'Milky Way'.

Our galaxy itself contains a hundred billion stars,
It's a hundred thousand light years side to side.
It bulges in the middle, sixteen thousand light years thick,
But out by us, it's just three thousand light years wide.
We're thirty thousand light years from galactic central point,
We go 'round ev'ry two hundred million years,
And our galaxy is only one of millions of billions
In this amazing and expanding universe.

INSTRUMENTAL WALTZ

The universe itself keeps on expanding and expanding
In all of the directions it can whizz
As fast as it can go, the speed of light, you know,
Twelve million miles a minute, and that's the fastest speed there is.
So remember, when you're feeling very small and insecure,
How amazingly unlikely is your birth,
And pray that there's intelligent life somewhere up in space,
'Cos there's none of it down here on Earth!

▶ **CD** track 8 (performance) track 9 (backing) track 10 (teaching)
▶ **CD-ROM**: audio-embedded lyrics/melody; slide show; lesson plan; piano accompaniment

ALIEN CONTACT

CHORUS

Is there life on Mars?
What exists beyond the stars?
Is there truth out there?
That's the X-file questionnaire.

ET ~ contact me.
Phone home, 'cos you're not alone.
Start Trek 'cross the galaxy,
Beam down to humanity.

VERSE 1

Creatures from the outer space
Visit earth but leave no trace.
Telescopes look to the sky,
Searching, list'ning, wond'ring 'why?'
Creatures from the outer space
Visit earth but leave no trace.
Visit earth but leave no trace.
Visit earth but leave no trace.

CHORUS

Is there life on Mars…

VERSE 2

What shall we do if we find a life form?
What shall we do if we find a life form?
Just say 'Hi mate!'
What shall we do if we find a life form?
What shall we do if we find a life form?
Communicate! Communicate!
Communicate! Communicate!
Communicate! Communicate!

CHORUS

Is there life on Mars…

VERSE 3

Ten green Martians, walking round on Mars.
Ten green Martians, walking round on Mars.
But they all just vanished, they beamed up
    to the stars.
Are there any Martians left on planet Mars?
Ah! Ah! Ah! Aiy-ee aiy-ee ah! Aiy-ee aiy-ee ah! Ah! Ah!
Ah! Aiy-ee aiy-ee ah! Aiy-ee aiy-ee ah!

CHORUS

Is there life on Mars…

▶ **CD** track 11 (performance) track 12 (backing)
   track 13 (teaching)
▶ **CD-ROM**: audio-embedded lyrics/melody; slide
   show; lesson plan; piano accompaniment

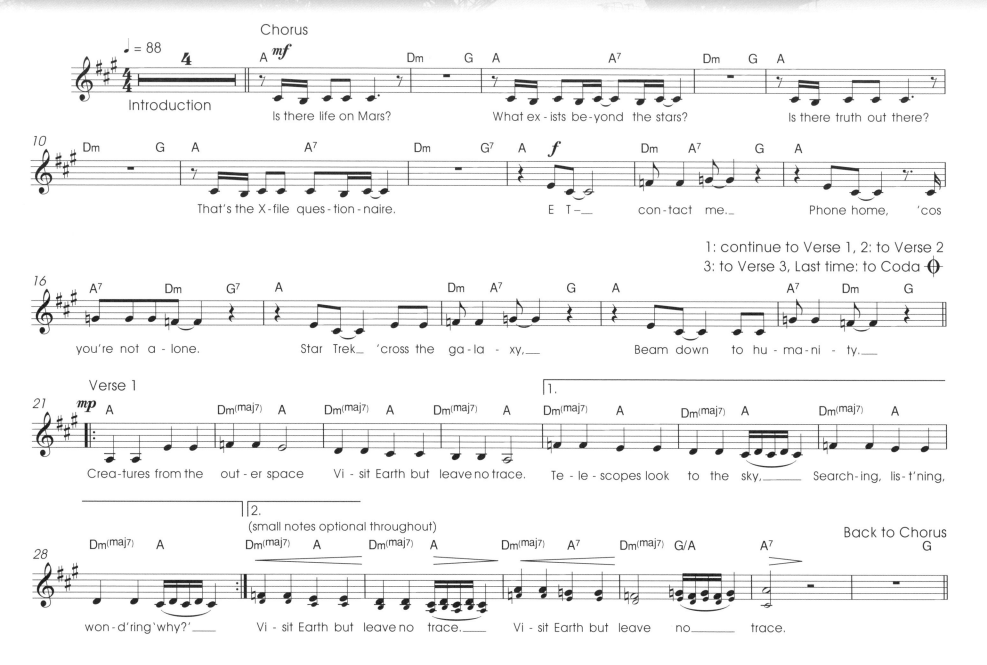

SPACE ODDITY

Ground control to Major Tom,
Ground control to Major Tom,
Take your protein pills and put your helmet on.

GROUP 1	GROUP 2
Ten, nine, eight, seven,	Ground control to Major Tom
Six, five, four	Commencing countdown engines on
Three, two, one,	Check ignition and may
Lift off!	God's love be with you!

This is ground control to Major Tom, you've really made the grade,
And the papers want to know whose shirts you wear,
Now it's time to leave the capsule if you dare.
This is Major Tom to ground control, I'm stepping through the door,
And I'm floating in a most-uh peculiar way,
And the stars look very different today.
For here am I sitting in a tin can far above the world,
Planet Earth is blue and there's nothing I can do.

INSTRUMENTAL

Though I'm past one hundred thousand miles, I'm feeling very still,
And I think my spaceship knows which way to go,
Tell my wife I love her very much, she knows.
Ground control to Major Tom, your circuit's dead, there's something wrong,
Can you hear me, Major Tom? Can you hear me, Major Tom?
Can you hear me, major Tom? Can you ~

Here am I floating round my tin can far above the Moon,
Planet Earth is blue and there's nothing I can do.

▶ **CD** track 14 (performance) **track 15** (backing) **track 16** (teaching: countdown) **track 17** (teaching: main melody) **track 18** (teaching: group 2 harmony part)
▶ **CD-ROM**: audio-embedded lyrics/melody; slide show; movie; lesson plan; piano accompaniment

IGNITION LIGHTSPEED

Take flight on a jet-black night in a rocket
   to the stars,
Get ready to zoom, straight past the Moon
   and take a left turn after Mars.
As the engines burn and the planets turn,
   and the light years slip away,
We'll be heading out to a purple cloud
   at the heart of the Milky Way!

GROUP 1

Ten!

Nine!

Eight!

There goes seven,
Wave goodbye to six and five,

Four, three, two, one,

GROUP 2

Prepare to fly, my friend,
Way on through space and time,
Time to accelerate
   across the heavens,
There goes seven,
Wave goodbye to six and five,
Let's hope we make it back alive,
Four, three, two, one,
World here we come,
Ignition, what's your mission?

CHORUS

Ignition, what's your mission?

Ignition, what's your mission?

Ignition, what's your mission?

Ignition, what's your mission?

Lightspeed ~

That's the only right speed.

Lightspeed ~

That's the only right speed.

Who knows what you will find, what wonders
   you may see?
When you take a trip on a big spaceship
   to the edge of the galaxy.
It's a mystery zone but it could be home
   to another form of life,
And when the ship descends, we could be
   making friends or fighting to survive!

GROUP 1

Ten…

GROUP 2

Prepare to fly, my friend…

CHORUS x 2

Ignition, what's your mission?

Ignition, what's your mission?

Ignition, what's your mission?

Ignition, what's your mission?

Lightspeed ~

That's the only right speed.

Lightspeed ~

That's the only right speed.

▶ **CD** track 19 (performance) track 20 (backing) track 21 (teaching: verse and countdown) track 22 (teaching: chorus group parts)
▶ **CD-ROM**: audio-embedded lyrics/melody; slide show; lesson plan; piano accompaniment

Acknowledgements

The author and publishers would like to thank the following for the use of copyright works in this collection:

Ben Glasstone for **Ignition Lightspeed** © 2011. First published in Singing Express 4 by A&C Black Publishers Ltd.

Matthew Holmes for **Sun blast** © 2012. First published in this collection by A&C Black Publishers.

Stephen Chadwick for **Footprints on the moon** © 2012. Based on Clair de Lune by Claude Debussy and including transcripts made available by NASA. First published in this collection by A&C Black Publishers.

Hal Leonard Corporation for **The Galaxy Song** by Eric Idle and John DuPrez © 1983 Kay-Gee Bee Music Ltd and EMI Virgin Music Ltd. All rights controlled and administered by EMI Virgin Songs, Inc. All rights reserved. International copyright secured. Used by permission.

Stephen Chadwick for **Alien Contact** © 2004. Used by permission.

Bucks Music Group Ltd for **Space Oddity** words and music by David Bowie. Published by Onward Music Ltd, Onward House, 11 Uxbridge Street, London W8 7TQ. Used by permission.

Every effort has been made to trace and acknowledge copyright holders. If any right has been omitted, the Publishers offer their apologies and will rectify any error in subsequent editions following notification in writing by the copyright holder.

First published 2012
by A&C Black Publishers Ltd
(an imprint of Bloomsbury Publishing Plc)
50 Bedford Square, London WC1B 3DP
© 2012
ISBN 978 1 4081 4708 5

Printed and bound in Great Britain by Caligraving, Thetford, Norfolk
Text and music arrangements by Stephen Chadwick © 2012 Stephen Chadwick
Lesson plans by Maureen Hanke
Cover image © Shutterstock Images LLC
Inside images (Alien contact title, Ignition, Space Oddity title, Sun Blast) © Shutterstock Images LLC; (The Galaxy Song, Footprints on the Moon, Space Oddity) © NASA.
Movies © NASA.

Series edited and developed by Sheena Roberts
Designed by Saffron Stocker

Music edited by Emily Wilson
Music setting by Jeanne Roberts
Powerpoint slide shows prepared by Michelle Daley
Sound engineering by Stephen Chadwick
Post-production by Ian Shepherd of Mastering Media Ltd